HOW
TO
GUESS
YOUR
AGE

How to guess your age

BY COREY FORD

///

ILLUSTRATED BY GLUYAS WILLIAMS

INTRODUCTION BY EDWARD STREETER

DOUBLEDAY & COMPANY, INC., GARDEN CITY, NEW YORK, 1950

FOR PEOPLE MY AGE
Cheer up, you're only old once

INTRODUCTION

Several months ago Corey Ford wrote an article on growing old in which he noted some odd changes which seemed to be taking place in his immediate environment as he neared the sixty mark.

Immediately thousands of people, who were sure Corey's observations did not apply to THEM, made thousands of copies and sent them to friends to whom they DID apply. At last, in order to lighten the load for a legion of overworked stenographers, Corey decided to put the article into more transmittable form.

This whole question of growing old seems to be a confusing one to most people. My interest in it is impersonal, of course, but nonetheless genuine, for I find nothing more depressing than to watch the physical and mental senility which seems to be creeping over so many of my contemporaries.

It makes me realize that in the inevitable process of time some of these things will probably happen to me. In fact during the last few years I have had a few rather disagreeable experiences along these lines.

For instance, take the matter of overweight. Personally, I have been so busy recently that I haven't had time to exercise as regularly as I used to. As a result I have put on about twenty temporary but nonetheless inconvenient pounds as all my suits are now too small. I'm not giving them away, though, because this is weight I can knock off whenever I find time to concentrate on it. Then I suppose it's going to be an equal nuisance having everything taken in again.

Also there are times when I catch a side view of myself in the bathroom mirror that would be depressing if I didn't know I was going to get myself back in shape shortly. Of course a lot of it is just the way one happens to be standing. By taking a deep breath and sucking in hard it's not so bad—not bad at all considering some of the freaks I have to look at every day.

I'll admit that for the moment I don't chop wood or climb mountains or shovel snow or take hikes or play tennis the way I used to. But that has nothing to do with growing old. It's just because we sold our place in the country and moved to town. Those happen to be things one doesn't do in the city. When I retire in a few years I'm going back to the country. Then I expect to take up the old life right where I left off.

Perhaps I've just been lucky. There's no question about it, though, a lot of my contemporaries are in dreadful shape. I used to go to a gym every afternoon, but the sight of them depressed me so that I gave it up. That was foolish, of course. I must call up the Swedish fellow who runs that place and arrange to start in again—if I can ever find the time.

Edward Streeter

HOW

TO

GUESS

YOUR

AGE

It seems to me that they are building staircases steeper than they used to. The risers are higher, or there are more of them, or something.

Maybe this is because it is so much farther to-day from the first floor to the second floor, but I've noticed it is getting harder to make two steps at a time any more. Nowadays it is all I can do to make one step at a time.

Another thing I've noticed is the small print they're using lately. Newspapers are getting farther and farther away when I hold them, and I have to squint to make them out.

The other day I had to back halfway out of a telephone booth in order to read the number on the coin box. It is obviously ridiculous to suggest that a person my age needs glasses, but the only other way I can find out what's going on is to have somebody read aloud to me, and that's not too satisfactory because people speak in such low voices these days that I can't hear them very well.

Everything is farther than it used to be. It's twice the distance from my house to the station now, and they've added a fair-sized hill that I never noticed before.

The trains leave sooner too. I've given up running for them, because they start faster these days when I try to catch them.

You can't depend on timetables any more, and it's no use asking the conductor. I ask him a dozen times a trip if the next station is where I get off, and he always says it isn't. How can you trust a conductor like that?

Usually I gather up my bundles and put on my hat and coat and stand in the aisle a couple of stops away, just to make sure I don't go past my destination. Sometimes I make doubly sure by getting off at the station ahead.

A lot of other things are different lately. Barbers no longer hold up a mirror behind me when they've finished, so I can see the back of my head, and my wife has been taking care of the tickets lately when we go to the theater.

They don't use the same material in clothes any more, either. I've noticed that all my suits have a tendency to shrink, especially in certain places such as around the waist or in the seat of the pants,

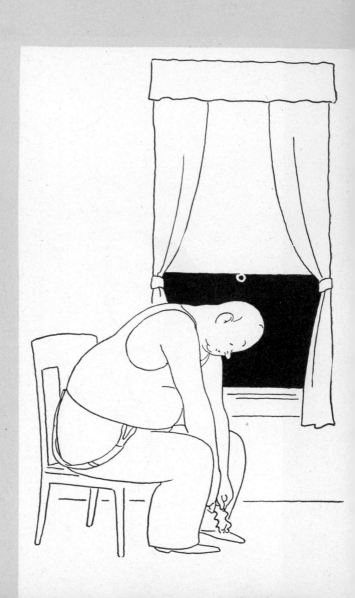

and the laces they put in shoes nowadays are harder to reach.

Revolving doors revolve much faster than they used to. I have to let a couple of openings go past me before I jump in, and by the time I get up nerve enough to jump out again I'm right back in the street where I started. It's the same with golf. I'm giving it up because these modern golf balls they sell are so hard to pick up when I stoop over. I've had to quit driving, too; the restrooms in filling stations are getting farther and farther apart. Usually I just stay home at night and read the papers, particularly the obituary columns. It's funny how much more interesting the obituary columns have been getting lately.

Even the weather is changing. It's colder in winter, and the summers are hotter than they used to be. I'd go away, if it wasn't so far. Snow is heavier when I try to shovel it,

and I have to put on rubbers whenever I go out, because rain today is wetter than the rain we used to get. Draughts are more severe too. It must be the way they build windows now.

People are changing too. For one thing, they're younger than they used to be when I was their age. I went back recently to an alumni reunion at the college I graduated from in 1943—that is, 1933—I mean, 1923—

and I was shocked to see the mere tots they're admitting as students these days. The average age of the freshman class couldn't have been more than seven. They seem to be more polite than in my time, though; several undergraduates called me "Sir," and one of them asked me if he could help me across the street.

On the other hand, people my own age are so much older than I am. I realize that my generation is approaching middle age (I define middle age roughly as the period between 21 and 110) but there is no excuse for my classmates tottering into a state of advanced senility. I ran into my old roommate at the bar, and he'd changed so much that he didn't recognize me. "You've put on a little weight, George," I said.

"It's this modern food," George said. "It seems to be more fattening."

"How about another martini?" I said. "Have you noticed how much weaker the martinis are these days?"

"Everything is different," said George. "Even the food you get. It's more fattening."

"How long since I've seen you, George?" I said. "It must be several years."

"I think the last time was right after the election," said George.

"What election was that?"

George thought for a moment. "Harding."

I ordered a couple more martinis. "Have you noticed these martinis are weaker than they used to be?" I said.

"It isn't like the good old days," George said. "Remember when we'd go down to the speak, and order some Orange Blossoms, and maybe pick up a couple of flappers? Boy, could they neck! Hot diggety!"

"You used to be quite a cake-eater, George," I said. "Do you still do the Black Bottom?"

"I put on too much weight," said George. "This food nowadays seems to be more fattening."

"I know," I said, "you mentioned that just a minute ago."

"Did I?" said George.

"How about another martini?" I said. "Have you noticed the martinis aren't as strong as they used to be?"

"Yes," said George, "you said that twice before."

"Oh," I said. . . .

I got to thinking about poor old George while I was shaving this morning, and I stopped for a moment and looked at my own reflection in the mirror.

They don't seem to use the same kind of glass in mirrors any more.